THE UNKIND COMPANION
—
LEARNING TO LIVE WITH LOSS

THE UNKIND COMPANION

—

LEARNING TO LIVE WITH LOSS

THE WIDOW'S MIGHT TRILOGY
BOOK ONE

MARLO PEDDYCORD FRANCIS

TATE PUBLISHING & *Enterprises*

 TATE PUBLISHING
& *Enterprises*

Tate Publishing is committed to excellence in the publishing industry. Our staff of highly trained professionals, including editors, graphic designers, and marketing personnel, work together to produce the very finest books available. The company reflects the philosophy established by the founders, based on Psalms 68:11,

"THE LORD GAVE THE WORD AND GREAT WAS THE COMPANY OF THOSE WHO PUBLISHED IT."

If you would like further information, please contact us:
1.888.361.9473 | www.tatepublishing.com
TATE PUBLISHING & *Enterprises*, LLC | 127 E. Trade Center Terrace
Mustang, Oklahoma 73064 USA

The Unkind Companion: Learning to Live with Loss
Copyright © 2007 by Marlo Peddycord Francis. All rights reserved.
This title is also available as a Tate Out Loud product.
Visit www.tatepublishing.com for more information

No part of this publication may be reproduced, stored in a retrieval system or transmitted in any way by any means, electronic, mechanical, photocopy, recording or otherwise without the prior permission of the author except as provided by USA copyright law.

Scripture quotations marked "KJV" are taken from the *Holy Bible, King James Version,* Cambridge, 1769. Used by permission. All rights reserved.

Scripture quotations marked "TLB" are taken from *The Living Bible* / Kenneth N. Taylor: Tyndale House, © Copyright 1997, 1971 by Tyndale House Publishers, Inc. Used by permission. All rights reserved.

Scripture quotations marked "NIV" are taken from the *Holy Bible, New International Version*®, Copyright © 1973, 1978, 1984 by International Bible Society. Used by permission of Zondervan Publishing House. All rights reserved.

Scripture quotations marked "NLT" are taken from *Holy Bible, New Living Translation,* Copyright © 1996. Used by permission of Tyndale House Publishers, Inc. All rights reserved.

Chapter six includes lyrics from Paris, Twila's "I Will Listen." *Where I Stand.* Sparrow Records. 1996.

The opinions expressed by the author are not necessarily those of Tate Publishing, LLC.

This book is designed to provide accurate and authoritative information with regard to the subject matter covered. This information is given with the understanding that neither the author nor Tate Publishing, LLC is engaged in rendering legal, professional advice. Since the details of your situation are fact dependent, you should additionally seek the services of a competent professional.

Book design copyright © 2007 by Tate Publishing, LLC. All rights reserved.

Cover design by Leah LeFlore
Interior design by Elizabeth A. Mason

Published in the United States of America

ISBN: 978-1-6024726-5-5
07.02.07

DEDICATION

I dedicate this book to my late husband, Capt. James Richardson Peddycord and my late father-in-law Mr. Jimmie Ray Peddycord. May the pages that follow not only serve to honor their memories but also serve to bless those who have encountered loss in their own personal way.

HONORABLE TRIBUTE

I would like to take this unique opportunity to pay tribute to the countless families that make up our nation's military community. There are no words eloquent enough to express my thanks for what you willingly sacrifice on a daily basis. Thank you, too, for reaching out and ministering to me when the folded flag was placed into *my* hands. At that very instant...for just a brief moment... my grief was eclipsed by a greater emotion, and that emotion was *pride*. I pray that this book is able to give back, in some way, just a portion of what you have given to me.

ACKNOWLEDGMENTS

I would like to begin by thanking my priceless husband and fearless leader, Steve. You have selflessly supported and encouraged my ministry from the very beginning. So many others would have never been so gracious, yet you always joyfully say, "But hey, I'm the *end* of this story. How could I not love that?" Thank you for always looking with spiritual eyes. "Lord, my heart's found a home"...and it's you. I love you with every fiber of my being.

To my precious children—Benny-with-a-Cowlick, Curly-Top Bradley, and Mary-Marlowe Mouse. You three are the complete fulfillment of my heart's desire to be a mother. Thank you for supplying me with endless joy and for keeping me grounded in what God has given as my highest calling. You are the best investment I will *ever* make.

To my Godly parents—Bill and Jewel Applewhite. This story has and always will begin with you. The consistent lives you led before me made choosing Christ the most desirable option possible. Thank you for the examples of Him in our every day lives. Thank you, too, for standing by me and supporting me when my knees grew weak and my heart broke into pieces. Next to God, your love has been the most unconditional I've ever known. I will never be able to thank you enough.

To my precious sisters and their families—Mabes&Co. and Donna&Co. One of the greatest joys in my life is how our whole family functions as one huge immediate family—intimately intertwined and in everybody's business. We are no doubt Greek at heart. "What, you're not hungry? That's all right...I'll get you something to eat." (smile) Your places in this story are marked on my heart in permanent ink...and I love each one of you more than I can say. Oh, and Katie...thanks for pointing out the path and greener pastures beyond the grave. What a beautiful observance to make ~ and how profoundly accurate to this story. (big smile)

To Rick's family—We have all experienced this pain from different perspectives, and I pray that this book will minister to your hearts as you recount our loss though written word. My desire has remained to honor God, Rick, and Pop through my ministry and manuscripts; and I hope you will feel that in the pages that follow. I send each one of you my most sincere prayers for a peaceful and joyful life.

To Dee-Dee—heartfelt thanks goes out to you for your excitement and support for all my ministry endeavors. Thank you, too, for your swipe at some early proofing for this manuscript—it helped a lot. I am very thankful for the relationship God is building between us. You are not only the mother of my husband...you are also my friend. I love you.

To *all* of my wonderful friends—if only I had the

room to write each one of your names individually. Whether God sent you to bless me in my greatest hours of need or sent you in years since to bless my here and now...I love *each one of you,* and I thank you for the selfless investments you've made in my life and ministry. Like I've said before, "Friends are the flowers amongst the weeds of life." God has given me a huge garden full of you, and it's beautiful.

To Ginger Plowman—I had to mention you by name because you have played such a direct role in the life of my ministry work. Thank you for so often putting me ahead of your own personal deadlines, *and* for always encouraging me to take the next step that presented itself. Your friendship and love have truly been a surprise gift from the Lord. I look forward to all the coming years of being "Girls at Heart" with you. I love you.

To Tate Publishing—Words cannot express how thankful I am that God found a home for my books in Mustang, Oklahoma! You have opened a door that has allowed me to experience a little more of what God has dreamed for me, and I had no idea how incredible that experience would feel. Thank you for having enough faith in these manuscripts to back them with your resources. May you be blessed and may God be glorified!

Most of all, I am honored and blessed to thank my precious Lord Jesus. Had Your love not pursued me, bought me, held me, and blessed me, I would have never experienced this life I love so much. Thank you, dear Lord, for giving me this story to share and for the opportunity to have it available to minister to others. This journey has been breathtaking, and had it not been for Your warm blanket of grace to warm me, I would have surely frozen along the way. I am Yours... for always.

TABLE OF CONTENTS

Author's Disclaimer for Advice:	13
Author's Note	14
Stark Reality	17
In the Beginning	21
Till Death Do Us Part	31
Wrestling with the Monster	39
Darkest Day	47
I Will Listen	59
First Hurdles	69
Visitation	79
No Regrets	89
Closure	99

AUTHOR'S DISCLAIMER FOR ADVICE:

The purpose of this book is to encourage those who are grieving and in need of something to let them know that they are not alone in their pain. My desire is to accomplish this by sharing my own experience with grief and the tools that allowed me freedom after devastating circumstances. I am not a trained counselor, nor do I hold a degree in the psychology or counseling fields. I am simply an ordinary person who found herself, suddenly, in an extraordinary place. Some of my advice is based on professional counsel I had while grieving, some is based solely on my own personal journey, and still some is based on the fact that I regularly travel and speak to large groups on this topic. I have gleaned much knowledge from the experiences of others. All advice given in the following pages is strictly my advice to you as someone who has lived it. If you find that you are in need of more help than these books provide, please seek out a professionally trained counselor or minister to guide you to the resource you require for your individual need. May God bless you in your current quest for peace.

— AUTHOR'S NOTE —

What do you do when your worst nightmare unfolds right before your very eyes? What do you do when all that you have planned for and dreamed about unravels in one heartbeat? What do you do when you feel something precious slipping out of your grasp and all you can do is watch it go—helplessly watch it go?

These are the questions that no one wants the opportunity to answer. These are the things our hearts try feverishly to avoid, yet somehow—at some point—most of us will find our hearts in that broken place of void and helplessness. What then?

The human truth is that loss comes to all of us in some way and at some time in our lives. The forms loss takes are endless, much as the trail of tears that fall from their cause. Loss comes on, many times, suddenly, and it leaves us feeling as if we don't even know what hit us.

Loss is the Unkind Companion.

There is really no one form that hurts worse than all the others, for when we are going through it, there's nothing we could possibly imagine that would hurt worse than our own present situation.

There is something that happens, however, as time passes. As seconds turn to minutes, and minutes into hours, hours into days, and days into years, the Unkind Companion, if entertained with a soft heart, becomes a living part of who we are. Not only that, but by God's grace and perfect provision in the heart of a Believer, loss begins to equip us with something that is priceless, and once gained, it is a mighty and valuable tool to carry into further battles.

Experience.

Once our *loss* becomes our *experience,* we can use it to help mend the wounds of others. We can carry it, much as Christ carried the scars on His hands and feet—a reminder of His past to bring hope to those in His future. We can use it to bring glory to the Father as we share our experience with others, but there is much to be done in the heart of a wounded child before his or her loss can be counted an experience.

It is my heart's desire that God will use my journey through the dark places of life to be a stepping-stone by which you cross over from that point of loss in your own life to that priceless, usable experience. In scripture, we see a widow giving her offering...all she had into the treasury.

> "And He saw also a certain poor widow casting in thither two mites. And He said, 'Of a truth I say unto you, that this poor widow hath cast in more than they all: for all these have of their abundance cast in unto the offerings of God: but she of her penury hath cast in all the living that she had.'" (Luke 21: 3–4, KJV)

There came a pivotal time in my life when I had to cast all the living that I had into the hands of the God that created me. I had to become that living offering in a way I had never known before. It was, ironically, during that same pivotal time that I truly began to understand what Paul meant when he said, "For when I am weak, then I am strong." Through God's grace and provision, my mite became my might.

We each have our own unique course to travel—our own path to pursue; but in the pages that follow, for just a moment, may we take each other by the hand and walk it together. By His grace we'll finish the journey in triumph.

Because He Lives,
Marlo Peddycord Francis

STARK REALITY

"And now, dear brothers, I want you to know what happens to a Christian when he dies so that when it happens, you will not be full of sorrow, as those are who have no hope." (1Thessalonians 4:13, TLB)

"It was Rick and Jim...it *was* their airplanes, and neither one of them survived."

These were the words I never wanted to hear. These are the words that burned in my ears as my brother-in-law confirmed what the television reporters were broadcasting. These were the words I heard in a crowded living room full of people busily trying to protect me from the truth. These were the words that would change my life forever—for Rick was my precious husband, and Jim was my father-in-law—and as quickly as he had entered my world when I was but a girl, Rick exited it, leaving a gaping hole in my heart and in my life.

This one moment of tragedy came out of nowhere and pillaged my existence in mere seconds. Something that hurts that deeply should take more time. An event that shatters your dreams, steals your future, and crushes your spirit should have to take more time than just the breath it takes to tell you that your husband is dead. This puzzled me, bothered me, and irritated me, for this life I had busily been building and nurturing—patiently taking year upon year to establish—in one stroke, it vaporized. How is this possible? How can something invade your world so swiftly and leave nothing at all behind except tears and pain?

I don't know how it is possible, but I do know that it is quite possible. What is infinitely more disturbing than that is the statistical evidence that shows that it is quite probable. Truthfully, if you have lived many years at all, you have come to the disappointing realization that in this life there is an Unkind Companion that comes to visit far too often for our liking. You never know when it will show up. You never know how long it plans on staying. You never know where it is going to take you once it gets there, and worst of all no matter how hard you try, you are never prepared for how you will react when it comes knocking on your door.

The Unkind Companion I am speaking of is loss.

To the largest degree, loss never completely goes away, but it does go through a metamorphosis of sorts. Your determination, faith, trust, and soft heart before God will determine just what changes will occur in your own life where loss is concerned. To the person who shuts down, loses hope, turns away from faith, and becomes increasingly despairing, to that person, loss will become *bitterness*. This bitterness will stifle any chance for abundant living and will eventually, I truly believe, lead to one's death, be it natural or unnatural.

To the person who purposes his or herself to trust God in the darkness, to hang on to the cross for dear life, to determine that some good will come out of the pain, well, to that person, loss becomes *experience*. It is at this point that I truly believe God can take anything, whether it be minor by world standards or horrific, and make it a blessing not only to you, but more importantly, to others. It is then that you can begin to live again.

If you are reading this book right now, chances are loss has come for a visit. What are you thinking at this very moment? Did my mention of hopelessness or despair strike a painful chord in your spirit? Are you afraid bitterness is creeping in? It is not too late to reverse that!

Let me make one clear statement before we go any further: I am not saying that even the most determined spirit won't have moments of despair or hopelessness or anger...everyone will go through that. God equips us with emotions and it's expected that we will experience the full spectrum of them during our visit with loss. However, I truly believe that in the heart of the determined Believer, those emotions will only serve to bring us back to where we should be. In other words, they will return us to our Father's arms of understanding love, sobbing perhaps, but there nonetheless. That is a totally different scenario from the person who experiences these natural emotions and then decides to stay there indefinitely. To those who sit down in the midst of all the negativity and feed the anger, hopelessness, and despair...it is they that run the risk of ending up bitter. I will talk more on this later.

First things, first.

— REFLECTIONS —

ଓ How do you really feel you are dealing with the Unkind Companion in your life?

ଓ Do you feel comforted to know that it is okay to feel natural emotions, and do you understand the danger of camping out in unhealthy territory?

ଓ Realistically examine if you feel as though you are headed in the direction of victorious experience or stifled bitterness. What areas point you to that conclusion?

ଓ While this book series deals specifically with loss in the form of bereavement, loss truly comes in many, many forms. If you are suffering pain over something other than death, pray that God will use these books to set you free from every loss you are experiencing. Loss is loss, no matter what the form.

IN THE BEGINNING

> "Unless the Lord builds the house, its builders labor in vain." (Psalm 127: 1, NIV)

I wish that somehow I could speak to you as you read these pages right now. I wish I could know what things in life brought you in contact with this book. I have no way of knowing to whom God will direct this book, nor to whom He will use it to provide encouragement...but I know that even as I sit here and write, He knows exactly who will hold these pages in their wounded hands, and even better still, *He* knows the life that brought you here.

I want to dedicate the remaining chapters of this book to addressing the nature of the Unkind Companion I spoke of in the previous chapter. Although, as I just stated, I have no idea what particular loss you have faced or are currently facing, I do know this: loss hurts us all in strangely *familiar* ways, and though the intimate details may be as unique as the prisms of a snowflake, the underlying feelings are very much the same. Through traveling down my own pain trail with you, I pray that you will feel that familiarity and find hope for your own unique circumstances.

I feel that in order to share with you from the perspective of where I have ended up in life that I must tell you about where I have been—who I am and how I got here. I suppose the best way to do that is to start at the beginning. I will try to relate all of this as quickly as possible, but I am Southern, so I feel it fair to warn you, we're not short winded.

Once upon a time, there was me. Well, that got us off to a thrilling start didn't it? Trust me; the bells and whistles come later, I have to build. It's what writers are supposed to do.

I was born in the suburbs of Chicago where my family was residing at the time. Daddy was a shoe salesman, and his North Carolina-based employer had sent our intensely Southern family up there to win the Midwest over, armed with little more than Daddy's winning personality and thick Pender County drawl. It worked. The buyers literally bought shoes from him just to hear him talk. Some would even call other people they knew to come in the store while he was there, just to hear him talk. So, talk he did, and sell he did...enough so, that in record time my family was moved back to the company's headquarters in North Carolina where Daddy was promptly made an executive vice-president of sales. Not bad.

I have two older sisters, and for vanity's sake I won't share publicly just how much older; but suffice it to say...*they're older*. Sorry, Sharon and Donna, that's the best I can do. Between the two of them, they have covered every base of being the most incredible older sisters any girl could possibly have. (Well, that is, if you are willing to overlook the whole "weekly stripping off Marlo's ruffled panties and hanging them over the living room door while hysterical laughter ensued at Marlo's expense nearly leaving her scarred for life" incidents.) What? Did you two *actually* think I would have a book published nationally and not bring that up? I've been waiting 32 years to get you back, and this seemed the most delightful way possible. I hope you are both thoroughly ashamed of yourselves. The whole world knows of your dark deeds, and that's good enough revenge for *this* little sister. There, now I've made my peace. We can move on. (smile)

All kidding aside, they both serve very definite roles in my life, and always have. Sharon is without a doubt the coolest and funniest person I have ever known. She has and always will be in a category totally and unequivocally all her own. To be honest, I haven't called her by the name, Sharon, since 1986. So, from here on out, I will refer to her as Mabes. I won't go into how she got that name, but you can be sure that the story is cool *and* funny.

Donna, on the other hand, I've always called...well, Donna. She, too, is in a category all her own. She is closest to me in age, and therefore it has been her footprints left most recently for me to follow. They have never led me astray. She is truly an amazing believer, a constant optimist, and a fiercely competitive Rook player. What more is there to add to that? Exactly.

My mother is and always has been the most devoted homemaker I have ever known. She maintained such an amazing balance in our home while Daddy was gone so much with a career in sales. She is present in every memory I have. Her commitment to making our house a home is one I saw her selflessly pursue with efficiency and passion. She is indeed, the ultimate female role model.

My earliest recollections of home are grounded and rooted in one simple word: *Security*. I always felt safe at home. We always felt safe at home. That is what Christ does to a home if He is made Cornerstone. I have always said that *this* is truly where my story begins for this is the root of it all; my salvation and life's direction came from the effects of living in my parent's home. I dare say that I probably would not be sitting here writing this manuscript at this very moment, had my story not started in that fertile environment. You see, I saw my parents live out their faith in their constant, every day actions—not just words, as so many people unfortunately do. They lived it out day after day after day. When enough of those days add up in a child's life, she begins to see a pattern—a way for living. She begins to see where to turn when times are great. She begins to see where to turn when times are bad. She begins to see where to go in each and every situation for strength, power, and life.

I began to see.

At a very early age I began to ask Mama and Daddy what it meant to be a Christian. They would share with me about what sin meant—the debt it carried. They told me about that dreaded day in Eden when Eve's decision marked all that would come after her. They told me about that mournful day on Golgotha when the debt of my sin was nailed to an old rugged cross. They told me about that glorious day when two women arrived at an empty tomb to learn from an attending angel that Jesus Christ had risen from the dead. They told me about a choice that I must make as to whether or not I wanted to give my life to that same Jesus.

Thank you, Mama and Daddy. Thank you.

It was at an evening revival service that the Holy Spirit called me to make that choice. I was almost seven, and with a purposed assuredness, I prayed that night to receive Christ into my little heart...and with a purposed assuredness, He invaded my life.

Thank you, Jesus. Thank you.

That night my journey began. I moved forward from that place a new creation. Granted, I hadn't been alive long enough to acquire any hazardous vices, but I was a new creation just the same. My debt was paid in full. I believe that the night I bent my knee at the foot of Calvary is the night my life was placed on a new path for all time. That night, God began to write my story, and He started it with a simple little girl who loved life intensely.

I always had an enormous imagination, which I always credited to the fact that my sisters were so much older than me, *and* that I spent most of my childhood playing with our poodle, Gi-Gi. I loved to pretend, and most afternoons found me either solving a crime as one of Charlie's Angels, taking orders as my father's secretary, or standing on the bed singing to thousands of fans at my sold out concert while, of course, Shawn Cassidy waited for me backstage.

As childhood playtime began to make way for more mature things, I found myself standing on the threshold of adolescence, peering over into the land of makeup, higher heeled shoes, and the most wonderful of all attractions...boys. How could I possibly be this old so soon? It seemed like only the week before I had been completely content with tea parties and Mr. Rogers; now suddenly I was thinking about junior high socials and just exactly what I was going to wear to make me look thinner. There was one thing, however, that time had not changed—in fact, time had only served to make it more focused. That one thing was a sincere desire to follow God's will for my life. My prayer had remained that He would lead me on the path that was most excellent—the path that would take me to the places He dreamed of— the path made just for me. Little did I know the twists and turns that would lie ahead as I began the journey.

As you are sitting there reading about my early life, I want you to stop and reflect on your own early years. My hopes are that you, too, had a very healthy and Godly upbringing. I hope that reflecting makes you smile and feel all warm inside. I pray that every person reading this can say that their home was a safe haven; however, I am very aware that for many, this was not their reality. In fact, as I travel and share my story with diverse groups, be they Christian or secular, I find time and time again most people's hurt trails begin in childhood. If that is the case with you, my prayer is that God will use this time to help you heal from the battles of your youth. No matter how you grew up, or where you grew up, or even if you are still trying to grow up, God is there to soothe and care for those wounds and He wants to help you find peace. The loss you are currently dealing with could be affected strongly by your childhood years so you need to keep that in mind as we walk through the coming chapters. Little by little God can bring it all into focus for you, and if you allow Him to, He will. Let's stop here and pray that as we continue together, God will use our yesterdays, whether nurturing or difficult, to help us become all He knows we can be today and all He wants for us to be tomorrow.

Dear Lord,

As I sit here and write, I pray that You will be a comforting presence beside all who sit and read these words now. We can't truly have an abundant future until we have a peaceful past; so God, please encourage those who didn't have the childhood they would have dreamed of. May Your love massage the scars in the soul of every wounded child and may they see You as the loving, nurturing, caring Father You are. May those with wonderful memories use those memories to encourage those who don't view the past with a smile, and may we always use Your love to help bind up the wounds of those with weary childhood hearts. Thank You that in all things You are Abba.

In Christ's Holy Name,
Amen

REFLECTIONS

- What areas of your past made you who you are today?

- Whether they were pleasant or difficult, what memories of your childhood stand out the most?

- Have you allowed those memories to find a productive place in your life now?

- Happy memories should regularly be revisited, while difficult memories should be carefully dealt with so that you are victorious over their power. You would never want to repeat any negative experiences with those in your current life.

- Do you feel confident that somewhere in your past you have taken the time to open your heart and life to the Lordship of Jesus Christ?

- If you cannot look back and remember a time such as this, let me encourage you to consider doing it now. I promise you that you will never find a better friend, a truer companion, or a safer harbor than what you will find in Christ. Don't live another day without the freedom that knowing Him brings.

TILL DEATH DO US PART

> Now listen, you who say, "Today or tomorrow we will go to this or that city, spend a year there, carry on business and make money." Why, you do not even know what will happen tomorrow. What is your life? You are a mist that appears for a little while and then vanishes. Instead, you ought to say, "If it is the Lord's will, we will live and do this or that." (James 4: 13–15, NIV)

There are so many yummy details that lead up to my marriage to Rick. For sake of time and direction, I simply cannot share them all, but some of them are a must. For example, when I was twelve years old, I was walking to my parents' car one rainy Sunday after the morning service had ended. Just as I stepped out into the parking lot, a Buick Rivera screeched to a halt barely missing me. As my head snapped to attention, I noticed two young men turn around in the back window to see what all of the fuss was about. The two fellows were Rick and his brother, Jon. Suddenly, it didn't matter that my life had just been in the balance...it didn't matter that Mr. Peddycord was irritated that some pre-teen had just scared the pants off of him...and it didn't matter that more than half of the congregation was at a dead standstill staring at the whole mess. All that mattered to me at that point was that as my life had just flashed before my eyes...that blonde-haired, blue-eyed hunk was not in any part of it. Who was this new stranger in our church parking lot? Where did he come from? How old was he, and where did he go to school? Did he like brunettes? Answers...I needed answers! I decided at that point to do a very Biblical thing: I sent out my army of spies to see if I could take the land.

He did like brunettes. How providential.

When the magical age of sixteen rolled around, Rick, of all people, turned out to be my first car date. We went for pizza after Bible school one summer evening. Finally, I was old enough to date the young man I had been crazy about since the sixth grade. Oddly enough, once we started dating, I began to realize something about myself that, while it irritated Rick to pieces, didn't seem to bother me at all.

I was fickle. So sue me.

After "discussing" that on several occasions, we broke up. I assume you can fill in the sound effects for yourselves. Imagine slamming car doors, huffing, words like, "Well, I hope you find what you are looking for one day!" And, "Don't worry, I will!" Yeah, you understand. We'll just leave it right there.

Okay, fast-forward several years and several maturity levels. Rick was a junior at the United States Air

Force Academy. For those of you that aren't too up on your geography...that is a very long way from Asheboro, North Carolina. Rick was home for Christmas break, and I was on break from the college I was attending. He called while I was out, and asked my father if he could take me out before he headed back to Colorado. Daddy said that *he* would have to ask *me*. When Mama told me that Rick had called, how glorious it felt to stomp around the kitchen ranting and raving about his nerve in asking, and how I was going to relish the opportunity to say a big, fat, whopping, "No" when he called back. (Okay, maybe I was still working on that whole "maturity level" thing I mentioned above. However, I *had* made progress.) Funny thing was, when Rick called back, I said, "Yes." You can thank my mother for that.

Five months later, Rick proposed to me. We married a week after his academy graduation. How's that for making up on lost time? I must admit, I knew that I would marry him the night I got home from that Christmas-break date. Thanks again, Mama. Simply put, Rick was the Godliest, smartest, most capable, and cutest guy I had ever met. The truth was, I guess that in my heart, I had been his since that rainy day in the church parking lot.

After the wedding and honeymoon, we were off to pilot training in Texas. Overall, eight years of marriage brought us twelve different mailing addresses. It was never more than a few months in any one spot. The Air Force was a wonderful experience in most ways. There was always a new adventure right around the bend, and it was certainly never boring. Benjamin Vance Peddycord, our little man, was born in January of 1992, and oh, how proud Rick was of him. I'll never forget the sight of Rick as he held Ben in his arms for the first time. He was wearing the scrubs they had given him for the operating room and one of the legs was stuck down in his Red Wing boot. It looked just like how Andy Griffith's pants used to do on Mayberry R.F.D. Even thinking of that right now makes me laugh. Ben was a fulfillment of a dream Rick had carried since his parents' divorce when he was a child. He wanted so desperately to give his children a home in which they could feel totally secure. He knew that God would bless that desire through Ben's life.

Although so many things were so right during all those years, something in my heart was terribly wrong. There was a constant nagging fear that had begun to worm its way into my mind almost from the very day I walked down the aisle to become Mrs. Rick Peddycord. I would go through cycles of guilt and rationale, panic and prayer...over and over and over again. It didn't help that Rick was in the military and that every time he left I had to go sit with all the other wives while they briefed us on what exactly would take place if our husbands didn't return from their current mission. It didn't help that Rick loved to race motocross bikes on the weekends and surf alone when hurricanes were brewing off the coastline. You think I'm kidding? He saw hurricanes as nothing more than the perfect opportunity for "great waves." Okay, *whatever*.

It didn't help that I had grown up in a home with two sisters, a worrisome mother (okay, sorry Mama, I forgot that you prefer to call it "realistic thinking"), a tremendously cautious father, and a French Poodle. All of this combined, weighed heavily on my spirit and caused me much pain. I would pray and pray for God to take the fear from me—all the while not being exactly sure what made me so afraid. I just knew that somewhere in my heart, I was scared that I was going to be called to give Rick up early. I hated that feeling. Moreover, it was only getting worse.

Where have you been with your fears? Have you spent years as I did, with a nagging monster pulling at your heart? Did the loss you are currently facing come from out of nowhere, or did you have some emotional preparation as I did? Looking back now, I really believe that God was getting me ready for what I was about to face. I have talked to so many people who have had similar things happen in their situations, but many have not. Of course, it was in hindsight that all of this became clear. If you are just now in the initial stages of your loss, you may not have had enough time pass to see it all clearly. I do want to say this also. Just because you may have dealt with a fear relating to something doesn't always mean anything is going to happen to justify it. I am sure that many, if not all spouses of those in service-related occupations (whether it be military, law enforcement, or firefighter) deal with a certain amount of realistic concerns and fears when they know that their loved one could willingly be put in danger's way on a daily basis. For instance, I spoke recently to a beautiful young wife of a firefighter. She told me that she had dealt with such similar feelings to those I had described during my marriage to Rick. Her concern was that maybe God was trying to get her ready to lose her husband, too, and she was so frightened. She was afraid that even emotionally she might be pulling away from him for fear of losing him. The pain on her face just melted my heart, and I had to remind her that none of us are promised a single day. I told her that I couldn't completely assure her that nothing was going to happen to her husband if he was a firefighter, but I also reminded her that none of us are even promised a good report from our yearly check-ups. Whether or not God is preparing her for a visit from the Unkind Companion, well, only God knows. However, of this we can be sure: if we are His children, we will never walk into a place He hasn't already gone before us to prepare. He will never leave us or forsake us, no matter what.

No matter what.

We must never forget that His grace is great enough to carry us through the expected and the unexpected. We can choose to let go of the fears in life, and it is in the letting go that we find true freedom to live.

REFLECTIONS

- What things have pulled at your heart? Are you currently dealing with fears in certain areas? Do you have a sincere desire to let all of it go?

- If you are currently dealing with loss, has it been long enough now that you can look back and see God's hand at work—preparing you for what you were about to face?

- Remember those things and write them down for future encouragement. It will mean so much to you in years to come. It will reassure you that He is, ultimately, in control.

- It is important to always keep in mind that if we belong to God, through Christ, we will never walk anywhere He hasn't already gone ahead of us to prepare. He promises us that.

WRESTLING WITH THE MONSTER

"The cords of the grave coiled around me; the snares of death confronted me. In my distress I called to the Lord; I cried to my God for help. From his temple he heard my voice; my cry came before him into his ears."

(Psalm 18: 5–6, NIV)

In 1995, my most dreaded, and consequently Rick's most desired, assignment came down the line with orders to report to Hurlburt Field, Florida—this being the Air Force's Special Operations Command base. It was there that Rick had been assigned to pilot the AC-130U Gunship. Now this particular aircraft was just the object my growing fear needed to send my worry into warp drive. It is a dolled up version of the C-130 cargo plane, used mainly to transport goods and equipment in the military. The gunship, however, has that basic aircraft body, only it is mounted with the hottest firepower known to the Air Force inventory. Its purpose is simple...fly low and slow into enemy territory, carry out your "I could tell you, but then I'd have to kill you" orders, and then get out before anyone can get you in the scope of their surface-to-air missile.

Realizing that this was to be Rick's new job was difficult to come to terms with. I knew that this one airplane had been his dream since finishing initial pilot training, and for that reason alone, I tried to be happy. It was when I was alone that the fear would start creeping up on me, wagging its gnarly finger in my face. I would repeat my emotional emergency procedure over and over: fear, guilt, prayer, snatch-back...repeat. When I say "snatch back" what I mean to say is that when I would feel the guilt start because of my worry and fear, I immediately would pray that God would forgive me for feeling those feelings. I would ask Him to take them away, and I would ask Him to protect Rick's life. I repeatedly failed to see that I was praying in a defeated manner. Instead of opening my hands and heart in complete abandon to God's will in this area, I would pray, essentially, only to try to make myself feel better. Just as each prayer would leave my heart and start its way Heavenward...I would reach up with my spiritual hands and snatch it back. I would tuck it back down deep inside my spirit, and that is why I believe it continued to return to me with such increasing frequency. We should never pray solely to feel better. I see that now.

It was January of 1997 that I had a miraculous thing happen. It would prove to be one of the most spiritual happenings of my life.

Rick left our house one cold winter morning and told me that his flight would be over late, and he wouldn't get home until midnight. I planned my day accordingly and decided later that I would just vegetate in front of the television until he returned home. As the evening passed and night fell, I could hear the guns on the airplane echoing off in the distance. The bombing range was close enough to our house that the shots sounded like distant rumbles of thunder. The sounds faded and eventually came to a halt around 10:30. *Ahh, they're finished. He'll be home soon.* The thought crossed my mind as I went back to watching my show. Midnight approached and I waited to hear the key turning in the lock. I waited, but no Rick. I decided to go get ready for bed. I did the usual beauty rituals and used up a good thirty minutes. No Rick. I went and checked on Ben. No Rick. I turned the bed down and decided I'd just wait there, my eyes feeling heavy. No Rick. Suddenly, I heard a knock at the door—only, it wasn't the door to my house; it was the door to my spirit.

I dared not open the door; I knew all too well who was waiting on the other side. The fanged monster of fear was back, and it tried desperately to coax me into cracking the door just a bit. I resisted over and over as the monster knocked louder and louder...the minutes passing slower and slower with no Rick in sight. It was around 2:00 a.m. that the pounding of the door became so fierce I had to do something. My intentions were to just barely open the door enough to tell the monster to go away. Surely I was strong enough to do that. Before I knew it, the monster of fear had forced the door open, and he jumped on me, sinking those fangs deep into my heart. I lay there in the bed, and I began to sob. I gave in to the fear and worry once again, all the while feeling guilty for my lack of faith. I knew that beast of fear had nothing to do with my Precious Shepherd, but I was too weak and tired to fight him off. My imagination began to get the best of me, and the sobs grew louder as I thought of the possibilities of why Rick was so late. What if someone rang my doorbell and informed me that Rick's plane had gone down during the flight? What if they told me he was dead? It was honestly as if I was lying there grieving Rick's death. It was as if the dam finally gave way, and I was gushing with the entirety of all the years of being afraid.

It was in that moment of complete collapse, that I heard another sound. This sound quailed the monster of fear; and for a brief second, all was silent except for a voice that said:

"Do you trust Me?"

It was a simple question, but one that stopped me with all the power in Heaven. I began to cry out to God like I had never done before in my whole life. I started praying out loud, and with every word that poured from my heart, the fanged monster began to shrivel. Every syllable I uttered became a weapon with which to slay him. I was finally coming to the Father with my palms open... spiritual fingers stretching upward to touch Him. I was finally ready to let this burden go. I was finally at the end of myself.

Oh Dear Father, I come to You tonight, afraid, and alone. You know exactly what I have been feeling for all these years. You know exactly what I am afraid of. I have hidden behind excuses, and I have made allowances for the worry I have kept and fed, all the while knowing You are not the author of fear or worry. I know that You have me in the palm of Your hand, but I have still felt so scared that something would happen to change this life I love so much. You know that I end every single prayer before bed with a request that we all live long healthy lives. You also know that what I am really asking is for nothing to happen to take Rick away from me. The truth, Dear Lord, is that Rick does not belong to me, but to You. You created him, and You have given him to me for as long as You see fit. I bowed my knee to you when I was a little girl, and You know that I have always asked for Your will to be done in my life. I mean that still, but I know that what I have wanted was for Your will to also be what I think is best for my life... which is for all of my family to live to be very old, together. Oh, God, I am so sorry for trying to hold on and force my life into the direction I want it to go in. I want to tell You this right now, and I finally mean it with all my heart. I want YOUR will to be done in my life, and if that means that I am going to lose Rick at an early age...well, then I just ask for You to give me the grace to accept it when it comes. Thank You for loving me.

I love You, Lord, and it is in Your name that I pray,
                                                                           Amen

What happened in that moment was miraculous. When I said, "Amen" I experienced what felt like someone taking from my shoulders a shawl made of steel. It was as if the burden lifted like an early spring fog, and I was able to breathe again—fresh, cool air. The monster was gone, and I knew in my soul that he would never again return to me.

It was about thirty minutes later, I heard keys jingling in the front door, and in walked my Rick safe and sound. As his wide smile greeted me in the bedroom door, he said, "I'm so sorry I'm so late. We had to divert for thunderstorms, and I couldn't call you. They had to bus us all the way back from Eglin."

Well, I just burst into tears all over again...overjoyed that he was fine and overcome with my newfound freedom. He came over and sat down by me on the bed. Wrapping his strong arms around my shoulders he said, "Baby-doll, why do you worry about me so?"

I looked at him with a twinkle in my eye, and I replied, "You don't know the half of how I've worried over you. I've carried it for such a long time, but tonight I finally let it all go. I finally let my fear go."

And I did.

I have talked to so many people in the years since who have dealt with fears and worries in such a gripping way. I look back on how many years I wasted just holding onto something I thought I had released. It has taught me a couple of very important things about myself. One I mentioned earlier. I should have never been praying solely to make myself feel better. When we do that, we are somewhat reducing God down to nothing more than a genie in a bottle. In other words, I would pray thinking I was doing the right thing. All I was really doing was saying, "God, here I am and I am feeling miserable. Please make it go away. Please make me feel better, and by the way, if You're interested, You can do that by reassuring me that nothing is going to come along to pull the rug out from underneath me. Tell me that it's not, and I'll be okay." Whether or not that was what I was verbally saying to God, that is all I was truly communicating from the fear in my heart. We so often forget that He sees straight through all our smoke and mirrors.

It was when I sincerely prayed for God's will—nothing more—that I found true release from what had been holding me captive. That leads me to my second discovery. In our prayer life, we must desire God's will over everything else we could ever pray for ourselves. It is in praying for His will that we can ever hope to truly be free, and consequently, ever feel better. It is when we totally get authentic with God and we hold up our spiritual hands, palms open—stretching those fingers out to Him in total abandon—that He can exercise the ability to take the burdens completely off our shoulders. In my case, I believe He wanted to free me all along . . .

He was just waiting for *me* to learn a lifelong lesson.

REFLECTIONS

- As you look back at your past, can you think of any monsters that have followed you, just waiting to jump on you at your weakest moment?

- How have you dealt with them?

- Has your prayer life been based on solely wanting God to make you feel better in a certain situation, or have you to come to Him praying with your spiritual hands wide open?

- Spend a few minutes seeking the Lord about anything you may have stifled away over the years. Whatever the monster's disguise, God can give you freedom to move on and heal completely. He's just waiting for you to learn the lesson.

DARKEST DAY

> "The Lord is my rock, my fortress and my deliverer; my God is my rock, in whom I take refuge. He is my shield and the horn of my salvation, my stronghold."
> (Psalm 18: 2, NIV)

How truly precious the freedom of Christ is. How tethering and solid is the Vine that holds the branches. For the next six months I went on about my busy life, scurrying about in the daily routine, exhausted in the fullness of life happening all around me. I was experiencing the benefits of my surrender in January on a daily basis. The fear was no longer there nagging at me—stealing my joy. It had been eradicated from the shadowy places in my life, and God was keeping it away.

How timely God orchestrates the events in the lives of his children.

I say that because as I look back over the events that followed my surrender in January, there is no possible explanation other than God's orchestral timing. Little did I know that as that particular winter made way for spring, and then spring made way for summer, so the seasons of my life were about to change, and although the calendar said June the 4th, winter was about to set in...cold, harsh winter.

 We had been back in North Carolina on vacation for just four simple days. It was hard to believe that our week of leave from the Air Force was almost half gone, and it seemed as though we had just arrived. I've always hated how vacations feel that way. Wednesday began much like the days before it had. It was hazy and humid—just what you'd expect for early June in the South. We had spent the night at the Peddycord's farm and as always, Pop was up at the crack of dawn; this time readying two of his airplanes for an aircraft delivery later that morning. He had sold one of his vintage warplanes to a man in South Carolina, so he and Rick were going to fly it down there, and then return together in the spare. While he was busy with that, the rest of our family was in the kitchen getting breakfast ready. We were just sitting down to eat when Rick came clomping down the stairs dressed in his usual off-duty attire: Levi jeans, a t-shirt, a "No Fear" baseball cap, and his pull-on Red Wing boots. As I looked up to greet him, I was impressed with how extra handsome he looked that morning. His classic "All-American" look was enhanced for whatever reason, and I said, "Mercy, you look so good this morning!"

 He replied, "Just jeans and a t-shirt."

 I shrugged my shoulders and said, "Well, that may

be so, but you are lookin' mighty fine in them!" He gave me a big, toothy grin and then sat down to eat.

As we drank our coffee we also drank in the yummy feeling of the farm in the morning—all the peace and quiet of the countryside. It was very relaxing to just sit and have a little quality family time before they left. Our cereal had scarcely settled when suddenly, the back door flew open and in came Pop, excited and spouting off flying lingo that only Rick understood. Somewhere in it all, the rest of us figured out enough to know when they were getting back and when we should return from our day of shopping. As they passed out hugs and kisses to us all, I had a sudden pang of not wanting Rick to leave. Maybe it was because Ben had been sick the night before, maybe it was because he looked so cute in his jeans and t-shirt, or maybe it was something more.

The day went on as planned, and after I had dropped Ben off at my parents to receive a good old-fashioned spoiling, I went shopping with my mother-in-law, Gayle, and my sister-in-law, Jenny. After scouring the entire mall for bathing suits and summer clothes, we realized that the hours had passed quickly and it was almost time to head back to meet the rest of the family to go out to supper.

Gayle, Jenny, and I drove over to my parents and got Ben. He was still reeling from a day of total pampering from his grandma, and so it took us a few minutes to corral him into the car. As we drove away and came to the stop sign at the end of their street, we were shocked to find that the traffic was backed up and not only that, but emergency vehicles of every kind were screeching by us as we sat there waiting to turn onto the highway—the very one that that lead straight to the farm. My heart sank, and I felt a rush come over me. My pulse began to soar and I got that cold, sweaty feeling all over my body.

I looked at Gayle and said, "May I use your cell phone?"

She said, "Of course, but who are you going to call?"

I replied, "Mama." I called and asked if she had heard of anything that had happened down the highway, and she hadn't. I told her about what we had encountered, and she said that she would turn on the television to see if there was any breaking news. Before we hung up, I said, "Mama, pray. I don't know why, but something inside me is telling me this has something to do with us."

At the same time, both Mama and Gayle said, "Marlo, don't say that!"

I replied, "I'm sorry, but I can't help it. Even if it doesn't, pray for the families involved...because it's bad."

We hung up, and in a few minutes Gayle was able to make her turn. We made our way slowly towards the farm, and had gone about five miles when we had to pull over for more emergency vehicles to pass us. Again, my heart sank as I began to feel a sick feeling in my stomach. I started trying to call the farm, and then the airplane hanger. There was no answer at either place.

I called again, and again, and again...no answer. Just a few miles more down the road, we came to the place where all of the vehicles we had seen had turned off onto an old gravel road. It looked like an old farm road. Jenny spoke up from the backseat, "Well, at least they weren't going to *our* farm." While her simple thirteen-year-old reasoning seemed acceptable, I barely dared to breathe. I felt as if time was slowing down and the car was moving along at a snail's pace. It seemed as if we'd never get there, but at last, we pulled into the driveway.

The land was still and quiet. There was no one outside and as I looked past the house, past the runway, and into the hanger, I saw that it was empty. *Hmmmm,* I thought to myself. *They must not be back yet.* For a brief instant, I felt like maybe everything was okay and that soon they would come in and land; my brother-in-law, Jon, would get there, and then we'd all go to supper.

A truck turning into the driveway interrupted that brief instant. As it made its way to us, we recognized the driver as their neighbor from across the street. He had an ashen look on his face, and as he rolled down the window, he spoke with a broken whisper.

"Where are Rick and Jim?" he asked.

"Well," I replied, "The hanger is empty, so we assumed that they weren't back yet. Why do you ask?"

He responded, "I don't want to frighten you, but I was just watching the news, and they broke in to say that they had just learned about a collision of two small aircraft, just south of Asheboro off of Highway 42."

Gayle collapsed into the floorboard of the car, her

sobs piercing the symphony of late afternoon crickets. I motioned for Jenny to take Ben inside, and then I just stood there...frozen. My vision blurred, my chest tightened...I wanted to scream, but nothing would come out. I was brought back to reality by the neighbor asking if we wanted him to go to try and find out what was happening. I told him all that we had seen driving home, and he said that he would go right away and try to find out anything he could.

Gayle and I went indoors and I immediately went upstairs to the television to see if I could find anything on the news. Every single channel I turned to, for whatever reason, was snow. I couldn't get *anything,* which I now believe was nothing more than divine protection for my eyes. I then turned to the telephone and started trying to call my parents. There was no answer, which frightened me all the more. I found myself racing around the house, embracing Gayle, reassuring the children...and praying.

Oh God! Is he dead? Are they dead? Can this really be happening? I kept looking out the window, hoping I would see them both coming in to land...hoping they had heard about the crash and had gone to see it from the sky...hoping that I would wake up and this would all be a dream.

It was not long until the house started to fill up with friends and neighbors; my hopes dimming with each car that turned into the driveway. Soon, Jon arrived with tear stained cheeks and a breaking heart. Frantically, we exchanged information, and he was back out the door to get some answers to all our questions.

After what seemed like years, I saw my parents pull into the driveway, and I raced out to meet them, hysterical and needing their reassuring comfort. How badly I wanted them to hold me and tell me that it was all a mistake—that it would all be okay. For the first time in my life, they were helpless to tell me what I needed to hear. They were helpless to fix things for their baby girl. The shattered countenance on both their faces gave the verdict away. They were just as frightened as I was. All we could do then was pray, and wait.

In about an hour, Jon returned, devastated and grieved to tell us that, indeed, it had been Rick and Pop in the collision and neither one of them had survived. I dropped into the chair beneath me, trying desperately to shut out the words he had just spoken. I became numb and cold, and I felt everything tunneling in around me. Words came to my lips without a warning, and in a whisper only God, Himself, could hear, I said, "It finally happened."

Suddenly I was brought back to consciousness by the feeling of a little body climbing into my lap. My heart melted inside my chest as little Ben wrapped his arms around my neck. He spoke gently, "Mommy, the ambulance will fix daddy, won't it? It fixed him after his motorcycle accident; it will fix him now."

Tearfully, I cuddled him up to my chest and forcibly said what I had no other choice but to say, "Son, this time the ambulance can't fix daddy. He and Pop were hurt too badly, so God took them to Heaven to make them well again." The words stuck in my throat like thorns, and I felt the room tunneling in around me again. A friend took him off my lap and went upstairs to try and distract him until I was able to get my composure. I became hysterical at the thoughts of what this would do to him.

    I sat in that chair with all the activity going on around me...all the people...all the noise, and it was nothing compared to the tornado going on inside my head and heart. It was then that I looked past all of the visitors and out the windows of the great room. The sun was setting, a fiery red, over the runway. I stood without warning and said that I was going outside to see it. Everyone in the room immediately clamored around to help me, but I said that I wanted to go alone. I wrapped a quilt around my shoulders, and I let Mama and a friend walk out with me. Soon, Jon and Gayle joined us, and we all just stood there soaking up the last rays of sunlight. As I looked out across the runway, my mind's eye began to paint a picture for me. I saw all of Rick's dreams, and mine, floating up in the sky. I saw the house we wanted to build in retirement. I saw the grandchildren sitting on our knees. I saw Rick learning the family business from his dad and them working side by side. I saw us growing old together. What I saw there in the sky was beautiful. Suddenly, I saw those dreams, one by one, falling through the air and crashing to the ground. I saw them burning and ruined...just like those airplanes. Just like those precious men. How could this be? How could such a beautiful sky swallow up my future and all of my dreams in one fell swoop? How could that sun dare to set with my Rick gone? What was happening? Those dreams were valid, they were good, and they were what I thought God had for us.

God.

Where was God? I had been so broken, so stunned by everything that had transpired in the last few hours, I hadn't been able to look for Him. I had cried out to Him, but hadn't taken the time to seek Him out. I knew He was there...He must be there. As the sun tucked itself away behind the earth, I took one last opportunity to look out across the farm. It was there, in the stillness before the nightfall that I cried out, again. This time my cry was different. It wasn't merely the lament of a brokenhearted widow, but instead, it was the cry of a child desperate to find her Father's hand. As a young girl I had bowed my knee at the foot of the cross. I had received mercy for my soul and grace for my life. I had prayed all the years since for God's will to be done in my life. I had even prayed it just six short months before. So, here I stood at a crossroad. The uninvited, unlovely, unwanted, Unkind Companion had just imposed its way into my life, and I was now faced with a decision. Would I question the Savior of my soul, and turn from Him in anger and despair, or would I instead trust the heart of my Heavenly Father even if I didn't know what tomorrow held? The choice was mine, and I ran to Him as fast as my spirit could run. It was there, as the chill of night crept in, that I felt God reach out and wrap me in a warm blanket of grace. Yes, God was there, and He was there...*to stay*.

This is my account of the day that loss invaded my world. Even writing the details almost seven years later brings back every single emotion and feeling of the afternoon. If I were to let myself, I could so easily slip right back into the horror of the moment and shrink into a useless heap. It is only by God's grace and strength that I can rise above that urge to crumble. It is only by that same grace and strength that you will as well. Tragic events have a way of marking you with permanent ink—even the slightest remembrance can trigger a flood of frightening feelings.

I am sure that as I relive my story, you are sitting there reliving yours, as well. That is that strange familiarity I spoke of earlier. Our pain links us together in ways nothing else quite can. For that very reason, I wish so much that I could stop right here and let you share your story with me. I would love to know the things I felt that you felt, too. Likewise, I would love to know the details that are uniquely your own. I wonder what memory of mine served to reassure you that you are not alone in your grief...none of us are alone.

Have you lost a spouse? Have you lost a parent? Have you lost a child? Have you lost a brother or sister? Have you lost a friend? Whomever you have lost, I know they were dear in some way, and for that pain I am so sorry. You deserve a chance to relive that loss in your heart and in your mind. In my experience of talking to many people who are grieving, I find that some of them have yet to really relive the experience in their hearts and minds. It seems too painful to do...but I believe that healing and freedom can only *begin* when you dare to let those feelings out.

Let me encourage you to not read any further in this book until you find some time to get alone and relive your moment of *loss*. You may have some major regrets about the relationship that is preventing you from coming clean with the pain of your loss, and that is okay. We'll deal more with that later. What I want you to do now is put all that aside for just a little while and concentrate on how your loss made you feel. How is it still making you feel? It is healthy to allow yourself to be broken in your grief. Remember, as I said at the beginning of this chapter, *He* is the tethering and solid Vine that holds the branches. Trust that. If you are His, you are safe to examine every single detail of your horrific day. If your goal is working your way from loss to experience, I truly believe this is your first and most foundational step. If you are merely stifling your feelings, thinking you are being strong, it's only a matter of time before you crumble. Please, don't let that happen, for far too much relies on your response.

REFLECTIONS

- Have you been honest with your feelings surrounding your loss?

- Have you come to understand that reliving your loss now in an open and honest manner allows for a healthy healing later?

- Are you having a difficult time doing this because of hidden regrets in the relationship? If you are, know that we will deal with those feelings later. For now, you must allow yourself the room to relive the feelings—even if the regrets add to the pain.

- You can know that I will be praying that God will give you the strength to not skip over this very crucial step in the healing process. Honest feelings and healing must go hand in hand.

I WILL LISTEN

"The righteous cry out, and the Lord hears them; he delivers them from all their troubles. The Lord is close to the brokenhearted and saves those who are crushed in spirit." (Psalm 34: 17–18, NIV)

If you are reading this book in the wake of losing someone you were intimately close to, then you can certainly relate to what I am about to say next. There is a certain emotional "autopilot" that turns on when something horribly tragic takes place. Activation of this survival mechanism isn't a conscious decision; it is something that just happens, I believe, to protect our hearts and minds. I also believe that it is an extension of God's grace, because it allows us to function in what otherwise would be a totally debilitating set of circumstances. While I remember many of the details immediately following the confirmation of Rick's death with amazing detail, I also remember feeling like I was having what I would facetiously call an "out of body experience." Of course, I don't mean that I was floating around the room, hovering over the rapidly growing crowd of supporters, but I do mean that I didn't feel at all like Marlo. I felt glazed over—numb—but still feeling so keenly all the emotions of the moment. I felt as though many of my initial responses were being done by someone else other than me. I knew that I was trembling and crying and thinking and talking...but it was as if inside of me all of that was going on and I wasn't the one doing it. Do you know what I am saying? I am sure many of you are nodding your heads in agreement right now because I have talked with too many people who experienced this same phenomenon, only they were still struggling with how to describe it. Indeed, it is hard to describe because it is something that you have to live in order to really understand what it feels like.

After I came in from watching the sunset, I was taken back into the great room, where I was overcome by another shockwave of emotion. We had a team of local paramedics who had come when they learned of the news. Benny and Joy Beck were two of those who came to see if we were well taken care of, medically speaking. They found that both Gayle and I had gone into a state of shock, and as Gayle's blood pressure was going up, mine was bottoming out. They took us back and put us in bed—removing all but our most immediate family from our presence. They were finding that every time someone we loved arrived at the farm it was sending us into a repetitive spiral of anguish, and they knew that *we* would end up in the hospital if it wasn't halted. Gently and lovingly they worked around us for hours—instruments of His grace to attend to our wounded hearts. Thanks goes out to *all* those who helped us that day.

Of course, immediately, I wanted my family all around me, and they all got there as fast as they could. Donna's family learned of the accident after getting out of their Wednesday evening church service. Given that they lived almost two hours away, it took them longer to get to us then they ever would have wanted. I will never forget the look on Donna's face as she came through that bedroom door and saw me lying in that bed—a crumpled lump of brokenness. Her sweet face was disjointed in agony, and she fell on the bed and into my arms. We laid there and sobbed together without so much as a word between us for quite some time. The sobs were all the words we needed for those moments. That first night, she slept on the floor right beside the bed. I didn't sleep at all, but hearing her breathing in the stillness and the darkness brought me great comfort. Thank you again, sweet sister, for loving me so much.

By the time that first night had set in, I had Daddy bravely and diligently making initial arrangements and phone calls, Mama staying right by me and being the nurturer she has always been, and Donna crying with me and holding me as only a sister can. That was all amazingly comforting...but someone was definitely missing from the picture, and that was Mabes.

As all this pandemonium was going on back at home, Mabes and her family were on the West Coast finishing up a business trip. They had boarded the airplane to come home without so much as knowing a thing. Daddy knew that he had to get the news to them before they landed and saw a local paper or listened to the television for both were plastered with coverage of the whole ordeal. Daddy knew that he only had one choice. He called the airline and explained the tragedy to them, asking that they intercept them and relay the urgent message to immediately call home. The flight was long, and it was not until the next day that they arrived back in North Carolina. Upon landing, Mabes' family was escorted off the aircraft and into a private office where they called Daddy for the news. I cannot even imagine what their drive was like from the airport back to the farm. I remember hearing someone say from beyond the bedroom door that she had just pulled in the driveway. I was still bedridden and by this time, totally exhausted. I thought that I would burst with emotion before she was able to get into the house. Mabes has always been such a rock for our family during emergencies. She is always the one to keep the level head and come up with a plan.

―

I have a vivid memory of one summer day after she was married and living across town from my parent's home. I was in high school and was sleeping late on this particular Saturday morning. All of a sudden, my mother came running through the house, waking me in a total panic. As she came into view, she was holding a blood-soaked towel wrapped around her hand. She had been on the phone with Mabes while simultaneously trying to drain a huge glass jar of cucumber slices she was processing for pickles. As she drained and shook the jar, pressure built up behind the cucumbers. In an instant, the jar exploded in her hands, severing much of her right hand in the process. She instantly screamed what had happened into the phone and then ran for the bedroom. I was getting dressed to take her to the emergency room when we heard the back door slam and in ran Mabes, carrying a bottle of Bactene and a box of Band-Aids. In the midst of that chaotic scene, Mama paused at the sight and then burst into laughter. Here she was, bleeding like a stuck pig and Mabes comes in as if Mama had fallen off the swing set. It would have been like trying to patch the Hoover Dam with a piece of bubblegum.

Unfortunately, as she came running to me that day on the farm, it was, once again, not a wound she could fix with Bactene and Band-Aids. Oh, how I wish it would have been. Her presence immediately provided me with strength, and even though she arrived late, her love got there at the perfect time. She, too, held me and cried with me. She was very much in a state of shock and full of so many questions. To have been gone and then to have come home to such complete devastation in the family was almost more than she could comprehend. It was very therapeutic to talk her through the order of events...that being my first chance to relive the tragedy verbally. While it was extremely *hard* to do, I think it was good for me to begin that process of wording it all out like I talked about earlier. I remember how peaceful it felt, even in the midst of that horrible storm; to finally have Mabes *and* Donna both there in the room with me adding just the dynamic I was missing to finally feel stabilized. Thank you again, sweet *sisters,* for loving me so much.

The last real piece of that first twenty-four hours I want to talk about is my time with little Benjamin. I told you about having to initially tell him that the ambulance couldn't fix Rick and Pop. That in and of itself was more weight than I would have ever thought I could have carried. When they took him off my lap and carried him upstairs, I fell totally apart. I was so frightened for him. How does a five-year-old little boy understand losing his father and grandfather all in the same day? What would this do to Ben's budding faith in God? How would I ever balance being both mommy and daddy to him? Sitting there in my tears, I prayed what was one of the most desperate prayers I have ever uttered. I begged to God to cover Ben...to seal his little heart and to protect him from doubt and disillusionment in the days to come. I just didn't want something this horrific to change the little Ben we all knew and loved.

It was a few hours later that they felt I was calm enough to see him. He had been upstairs with his cousins and when they brought him to me and my initial instinct was to begin wailing again. I wanted to scream as loud as I could...but I didn't. Instead, I chose to focus all my attention on ministering to Ben's heart. My mind was racing, trying to find just the perfect thing to say to make him feel safe and comforted. It was then that he climbed up on the bed and nestled himself close to my chest. He looked up at me with those huge, blue eyes and he said, "Mommy, I'm going to take the trash out for you, and I'm going to feed Dixie every night, and..." his little voice trailed off in my ears as my heart grasped what he was trying to do. He was naming all the things he had observed Rick doing in our home on a weekly basis. From taking out the trash, to feeding our dog, Ben was essentially trying to minister to *me* in the wake of Rick's death. The realization of that blew my mind. What a little man, and what an *amazing* God that He was already giving me a glimpse of just how much He was going to seal Ben's life for a greater purpose. *Thank You, God, thank You.*

    Those first hours were incredibly horrible, to say the least. I know that surely in your own life, they were as well. Maybe you had a large family and many friends to come to your aid and comfort you with love and attention. Perhaps, you did not. Many people face hard times such as these with no one to help shoulder the burden. If you are one of these, may I offer you my shoulder on which to lean? While, obviously, I cannot offer you my physical shoulder, I can offer you my spiritual one. As this book is being written and infinitely more as it reaches readers in the future, I am praying for you and will continue to. Be reassured, knowing that right now while you are reading this you are being lifted up by someone who understands. I want to help you to shoulder the pain and I will ask God to seal *your* heart and protect *you* from doubt and disillusionment in the days to come. In this, I am reminded of a song written by Twila Paris. I have found much strength and encouragement from its lyrics:

> Could it be that He is only waiting there to see
>
> If I will learn to love the dreams that He has dreamed for me?
>
> Can't imagine what the future holds
>
> But I've already made my choice.
>
> And this is where I stand, until He moves me on, and I will listen to
>
> His voice.

REFLECTIONS

- What was your initial reaction in the moments following your loss? Did you feel the emotional "autopilot" come on?

- If you are currently going through the initial stages of your loss, are you able to express yourself to those around you? Do you have family or friends to help you sort it all out? If not, I encourage you to seek out someone to talk with, be it a minister or counselor. Talking really helps put your feelings to a peaceful rest.

- If there are small children involved in your loss, make sure you are talking to them and communicating stability and love to them. Try and keep as much routine in their lives as you can. Children adjust best when the lines stay the same, whether it's discipline or daily activity. Even if they appear strong, like Ben did, they are still looking for reassurance that everything will be okay.

FIRST HURDLES

> "The Lord is gracious and righteous; our God is full of compassion. The Lord protects the simple-hearted; when I was in great need, he saved me. Be at rest once more, O my soul, for the Lord has been good to you."
> (Psalm 116: 5–7, NIV)

As that first morning without Rick began to take shape, even before Mabes arrived at the farm, I knew I was in for a long and harrowing day. I had spent most of the night before staring at the wall of the bedroom. On it hung Rick's high school graduation picture and as each hour passed, the moonlight cast a steady glow on his face making it impossible to take my eyes off of it. I stared as his sandy colored hair and big blue eyes. I stared at his signature bright smile, and I was moved to observe that the years had not tarnished its brilliance. That was the same smile that had, just hours earlier, left me standing in the farmhouse kitchen. Just a few hours before he had been hugging me, and now I had to accept that he was gone for good. I had to accept that I would never see that smile again this side of eternity. I had to accept that dawn had come and I was going to have to get up and face the first day of the rest of my life without Rick by my side. How are we supposed to accept any of those realities? I honestly didn't know if I would be able to make it through the day alive. I didn't know if my mind and my heart could function within those limitations. Amazingly, though, I had made it through the night, and I would have never believed I could do that. I guess I was beginning to see what God's grace is, infinitely, all about.

As the sun began to rise, the room began to brighten. I could see Donna asleep on the floor by my side of the bed. Gayle lay restless beside me, and I was aware that the house, even that early, was already abuzz with activity. The numbness was beginning to wane along with my hopes that I would wake up and it would have all been a mistake or bad dream. I remember vividly feeling such a sinking heartache as I realized the morning had come and I hadn't dreamt any of it. Do you remember feeling like that, or even yet, are you feeling like that at this very moment? Sometimes things are so horrible, you just believe that when the sun comes up the next day it will have all been a huge mistake and everything is really alright. Doesn't it crush you when you find out it is not? Scripture says in Proverbs 17, "A crushed spirit dries up the bones" (NIV). What a true statement. Life's events can certainly leave us feeling parched.

In the dimness of the moment, my thinking began to shift gears. My initial thoughts had been consumed solely on the fact that Rick and Pop were dead. That is all that I could contemplate as the hours of the night slowly passed. That first wave of shock was saturated only with thoughts of whom I had just lost and how I would never be the same again. However, as the sun rose higher and everyone started to wake up, my mind began to turn to what I was going to have to do in the hours that would soon follow. I knew that there were so many decisions to make, so many feelings to consider, so many people to consider. I rapidly became overwhelmed with all that would have to be done in the wake of something this horrific. Just the list of people to contact was mind-boggling. How would we ever manage the details for two funerals, much less survive the emotions they would evoke? I broke down weeping again, just not sure if I was up for the task. How in the world was I to stand under a burden so heavy? It was then that I was immediately flooded with a wave of God's peace and grace. I didn't know how I was going to do it, but God whispered in my heart that I *would* do it and that He would be there in every moment. I didn't know how He was going to get me though the next twenty-four hours, but I did believe that somehow, He would. I took a deep breath, and decided to give it my best effort. The day had officially begun.

Even with all the help I was getting, there were many decisions that only *I* could make. What horrible timing. I was in no frame of mind to think clearly about anything, and yet, I *had* to think with keen precision to avoid any regret later. I wanted to make good choices—ones that I would be proud of in the future—but what an awful time to have to process anything. Most of you know exactly how that feels, don't you? Some of you have had the opportunity to make arrangements ahead of time, as with a long-term illness. While painful, that terminal foreknowledge gave you the ability to make provisions before they were actually needed. In the case of a sudden tragedy, like mine, the chaotic scenario is just compounded with the preparations that must be made. It seems an impossible task.

We all know how the list goes: Which funeral home to use, the time for the visitation, the casket, the clothing, the burial site, the service, the speakers, the musicians, the pallbearers...on and on and on until you feel as though you are going to either explode from the pressure or implode into a trembling heap of nothingness. While I didn't want to have to be the one to narrow down that growing list of options, a certain grace-induced adrenaline took a hold of me as we were being escorted downtown. I wasn't sure what emotions I was getting ready to face, but I was determined that no matter how difficult it might be once I got there, I would not let anyone else make those choices for me. I owed it to Rick to be strong.

I remember walking into the funeral home and experiencing this overwhelming sensation of mistaken identity. It was as if I was there for someone else—in someone else's place. The moment was so surreal that my mind, once again, tried to deny the authenticity of the accident. Although I knew beyond a shadow of a doubt that everything was true, in that instant, I went into a state of denial. I've often heard that as humans we can be put into situations where our minds shut out traumatic information. It is a very natural way to protect ourselves. For a short period of time, I think I went into that mode. It was as if I was standing there frozen, engaged in a silent argument between my head and my heart.

Despite all I had just experienced, I stood there not accepting that I was there to pick out any of these things for Rick. It had to be a mistake. If they could have just shown me his body *maybe* I could have been convinced, but because of the explosion, I was not allowed to see his remains. With no evidence for my eyes, my heart just locked up and refused to admit that I had to make any further moves toward a burial. During those moments of inner turmoil, I had to cross a *bridge of acceptance*. To walk into that conference room was to fully acknowledge that the bad dream wasn't going to end. Sliding down into that shiny leather chair and opening that folder full of glossy casket photos was crossing a bridge that I could never cross back over. There would be no turning back, and my heart knew it. The silent argument ended with reality and rationale triumphing over pain and denial. As I regained my composure and walked towards the conference room door, I felt the Lord take my hand and whisper words of strength, love, and courage into my spirit. Undoubtedly, the first step is always the most difficult.

Those were some of the very opportunities I had to offer Him "all the living that I had" such as in Luke 21.

I was totally bankrupted, empty, helpless. All that this widow had to offer Jesus was the two meager mites of faith that she had. Thankfully, it was enough to stir the heart of the Father. God was moved to compassion, and His grace fell on me in those hours like a warm blanket fresh from the dryer. It enveloped me and surrounded me in such a way that every other threat seemed to take a back seat. It was just enough grace to get me through the moment and on to the next hurdle—the visitation.

If you are in a similar position, the emotions I just described are no doubt, painfully familiar. I don't know what exactly makes your experience unique, but I am sure that this time in your process was very difficult. How could it not be? I failed to mention that this was one time I really *desired* to be alone. I remember telling my family to stay behind and that was a very hard request for them to grant. My mother, especially, didn't think I had any idea about what I was about to walk into, and she was right. I had no clue, but I was sure that I wanted some space around me to think. Some well-meaning friends showed up, despite my request and I had to remember that they only did what they thought was best. At the time, however, it really irritated me. I don't mean that to sound harsh because I appreciated every bit of support and love that surrounded me each step of the way. However, there was a few times, this being one of them, when I felt like people ignored things I would say. I am sure that they thought I wasn't thinking clearly and so their actions were based on what they thought was best for me, but the truth was, I knew exactly what I was saying and doing and I wanted people to respect the validity of my thinking.

There is a fine line to walk with people when you are ministering to their needs in situations like this because some people aren't capable of processing everything at once, therefore requiring more help than others. If you find yourself reaching out to those living through the first moments of grief, tread carefully as you weigh out whether or not they need you to think and act for them. If they do, then help them any way you can; but if they make specific requests that seem safe and they feel strongly about them, try your best to respect their wishes and give them the room they need to feel that they are in control, not being controlled. Do you know what I am trying to say? It's actually hard to put into words exactly what I mean by this. It's just that in this situation, it is already very easy to feel extreme helplessness. When you feel as though your voice isn't being heard by those around you and you are being patronized, it makes it all the worse.

On the other hand, if you are the one grieving and you feel that you need someone to be your voice and to help you process certain things, don't be afraid to admit that. You may feel one way one minute and a different way the next. You never know until the next hurdle approaches. When you find that you are in need of help, ask for it. If you *don't* need that help at a particular time, then express that as well. Just keep in mind that people are there because they care for you and want to meet your needs. Stay sensitive to their feelings because they are sacrificing something in order to be there with you. In my case, I never said a word to the ones who showed up at the funeral home, despite my wishes to be alone. I know that it was well-meant, even if it was irritating. It is all in the past now, and had I spoken harshly, it might have wounded them deeply. Even in our sorrow, we need to consider how those around us are feeling, too.

Unfortunately, as difficult as this day is in the life of the grieving, it is not even the tip of the iceberg. The hurdles just around the bend will be even harder to clear successfully. Thankfully, life comes just one minute at the time.

— REFLECTIONS —

- It is truly so important to remember that life comes just one minute at the time. That is exactly how you should approach it as you face your loss. In time, you will be able to handle five minutes at a time, then a day, then a month. Healing comes this way, but thank God, it comes.

- Be clear to those around you about what you are feeling, no matter what stage of grief you are in. You may need to rely heavily on those around you at times, and at other times you want some space. Make sure you communicate your desires in a sensitive, yet clear manner.

- Remember that the people surrounding you are most likely sacrificing something important to be with you. Don't ever take that lightly.

- When planning your loved one's service, make sure you keep a "no regrets" mentality. No idea or feeling is insignificant. Once they are buried, they are buried, so make sure you search your heart well when making these very permanent, important decisions, and don't let anyone rush you.

- Every step of the process that leads from loss to experience will feel like a hurdle because it is a hurdle. Remember to count each one as a victory and look back on them every day in order to provide extra motivation to continue the journey.

VISITATION

"That is why we never give up. Though our bodies are dying, our spirits are being renewed every day. For our present troubles are quite small and won't last very long. Yet they produce for us an immeasurably great glory that will last forever. So we don't look at the troubles we can see right now, rather, we look forward to what we have not yet seen. For the troubles we see will soon be over, but the joys yet to come will last forever."

(2 Corinthians 4: 16–18, NLT)

As that terribly draining day came to an end, I realized that even though it had been the most difficult day of my life, I had survived it. It was a small victory, but one that I took notice of—not that it helped much. As bedtime approached, I dreaded the thoughts of trying to sleep again. Because it had been such a miserable night before I resisted the idea of getting that still and quiet once more. I knew that I had no choice, so Gayle and I finally consented to taking something to help us sleep and we went to bed. Mama and Daddy had so many people, extended family mostly, coming to their house that I made them go home that second night to rest and to receive the comfort our loved ones had come to extend. They needed to feel connected to us, and we needed to feel connected to them. Mabes took sentry duty for the night and made herself a bed on the sofa outside Gayle's bedroom.

It might seem strange that Gayle and I slept together again that second night, but there was something incredibly settling about it. I think we felt identically seared by the accident, and for a few days, we wanted to be together every single minute. I felt that she was the only person on the face of the whole earth who knew exactly how I was feeling. Both Rick and Pop held many titles for many people, but for Gayle and me that title was *husband*. I would never have had her lose Pop, and she would never have had me lose Rick, but having each other to "walk through the valley of the shadow of death" with made those first days more bearable for both of us.

As we laid there winding down from the events of the day, we discussed many things, including all the decisions we had made about the visitation, the funeral, and the burial. Thankfully, we had agreed on every single thing that had come up. Perhaps the most difficult choice to make was where they would be buried. Amazingly, we were going to be able to bury them on the family farm, just as Rick had requested of me should he have ever been killed in combat. Gayle felt that Pop would have wanted the same thing, and so through Daddy's diligence to research it and get approval from the EPA, all the plans were a go to make it happen. It was a miracle and a long shot, but God worked it all out perfectly.

We also talked over the painful truth that if either one of them had survived the crash; they would have been a half-man for the rest of their lives. We agreed that it was merciful of God to take them together rather than to leave one with that kind of scar to bear alone. After our conversation dwindled, I felt the most at ease I had felt up until that point. Just talking through the day and feeling good about what we had put into action, coupled with being able to talk about the accident itself, brought me great peace. I actually slept a little bit that night—drifting off thinking about what the next day would hold.

When morning came, I awoke feeling different than I had the morning before. It hadn't even been forty-eight hours since the accident, yet somehow it seemed like so much longer. So many things had happened in that short amount of time. Things were more real with that second sunrise, and I felt like I had a better understanding of what to expect. I was aware that this would be the day I would be seeing many of the people who had played an important role in my life, and that frightened me a little. I knew that I had been so overcome with emotion that first night when I would see a new face come through the door. What would I do when I saw so many precious friends one after the other? I had to trust that God would help hold me together.

As the afternoon began, the doorbell rang with more frequency. One of the earliest visitors was my cousin, John. He had been trying desperately to get to me since he heard the news on TV. He had made several attempts to find me during those first twenty-four hours. Finally, that afternoon, he was able to get to me and just the sight of him brought me joy. Every precious person who came to support me brought me joy. Isn't it strange how we can be so broken and yet feel joy through Christ? I felt my strength grow with each familiar face that came into my view. I had been so afraid that I wouldn't be able to bear seeing my friends, but somehow God's preparation in my heart allowed their company to be just the medicine I needed so badly. By the time we had to excuse ourselves to get ready to leave for the visitation I had already seen many, many dear friends including my very best friend from adolescence, Cindy Snider, as well as Lori Cardoso and Steve Francis—both neighbors from Florida. As the limousine took us into town early, we knew that we would arrive in time to see the caskets and get our bearings before we received condolences from the rest of our priceless friends. We were certainly in for an overwhelming shock.

The visitation was to begin at seven and end at nine. We arrived at six-fifteen and were to be escorted into the viewing rooms alone to gather our thoughts and emotions. As we started into the back of the building we were informed that so many people had already arrived, the room was already filled. What took place immediately following that still boggles my mind.

I was lead into a packed room, each face intimately familiar to me. I was bombarded with kind words, tears, hugs—all the while trying to stay with the funeral home representative leading Gayle and me to our places to greet the visitors. I got disoriented and confused at the swirl of people around me, and I didn't know where to stand. I soon realized that my family had been escorted on to Rick's casket and I had followed Gayle to Pop's. When I realized the mistake I had made I looked across the crowded room and saw Rick's flag-draped casket staring me in the face. I felt my blood run cold as I felt humiliated and embarrassed to be in the wrong place. I wanted to run and hide, or better yet to blink my eyes and have the room to myself just long enough to react to the harsh reality of what I was looking at. As I staggered across the floor towards his casket, some people began to realize what had happened. I was far from composed as I made my way to where I should have been standing all along. Those who had realized the mistake kindly and quietly got me to my parents who were beginning to panic at not being able to find me. How thankful I am for those that meekly got me to where I needed to be without raising a fuss—a tender ministry, not overlooked.

 I don't think that I can possibly explain to you the way it felt standing there. Immediately, I had to start receiving the line of people who had come to offer their sympathies. I had no reaction time whatsoever as to what was sitting right behind me. Periodically, my dress would brush up against the pine casket as I would bend over to hug someone or lose my footing a little. For the first hour I was totally wearing the mask of protocol because all that was screaming through my head was the fact that Rick's body...the body I had not been able to see, was in a pine box right behind me and I couldn't even authentically react to it. It was horrible.

After the first hour or so, I began to settle into my surroundings. Benjamin stayed with me for just a little while and then a family friend took him to give him a break from all the grown-up emotion he was being exposed to. He had drawn Rick a picture for them to put in the casket, so once he was convinced they had done that, he was ready to go. After I knew he was taken care of and the shock of my entrance began to wear off, I was actually able to feel the precious outpouring of love that was very evident in that room. One by one each guest came by me so full of encouragement and support. So many friends came from so far away—each one holding a special, special place in my heart. I remember when Stephen and Debbie King arrived from Tennessee. They had been Rick's and my very closest military friends from the early days of pilot training. Those first months of living so far away from home had me desperate for a Southern friend. I'll never forget the morning they first showed up in our Sunday school class. They didn't have to say a word because Debbie's hair was as big as mine, and I said, "Praise God, my Southern friend has arrived!" In no time, we considered them family, not friends. They had been so devastated when Daddy called them with the news of the accident. Their arrival at the funeral home is one I will never forget.

The Rices, the Dunns, the Formans, the Downings... so many dear friends made the long journey to share in our grief, and God used every single friend and every single family member to accomplish a great work of grace in my life. Thank you, guys; you will never know the vital role you played in my sanity and healing. I love you all.

Needless to say, the visitation wasn't over at nine. Many times the funeral director encouraged me to leave and let family take over the greeting, but I felt firm in my resolve that the guests that stayed until the very end deserved to grieve with me personally. Gayle felt the same way, and so we stayed. It was over around 12:15 a.m. Ironically, the room I had earlier wanted empty was now completely still and somehow I longed for all the noise to return. Suddenly, I was almost afraid to turn around and face the pine box alone. I felt I needed rest before I tackled the emotions it would bring and so I decided to come back the next morning before the funeral and have my time alone with Rick then. Little did I know what a healing experience it would turn out to be.

In our modern society, people are more and more doing their own thing where funeral arrangements are concerned. The traditional means of visitation the night before, church funeral the next day, receiving family at the home afterwards, etc. is quickly being modified to meet many different criteria. Religious customs, cost, family dysfunction, convenience, personal preference— these are but some of the reasons people are making modified plans to what we have been used to in our country for so long. I even heard from a friend in the business that in some parts of the country they have drive-by viewings now. I can't quite wrap my mind around that one yet. Anyway, the point is, you may be one of those who didn't make conventional arrangements for your loved one. Your reasons are personal, just as your grief is personal, and I pray that when it was all said and done, you were satisfied.

As for me, I would have never realized the healing that takes place in a receiving line until I experienced it for myself. Once it fell into a rhythm, I felt my spirit drawing strength from each word spoken and each hug around my neck. Some told me stories about Rick I had never heard, while others reminded me of stories I had heard many times before. I cried, I laughed, I listened, I talked...and at the end of the night, all things considered, I know God used it to give me the strength I needed to face the next day. If you have hesitated in the past, thinking that if and when it is *you* making the arrangements for someone you love, that a receiving line isn't something you would want to have, I would encourage you to reconsider. Out of everything that happened in those first few days, I gained the most strength, love, and support from those who came and waited through that line. Face to face time evokes immeasurable power.

—— REFLECTIONS ——

- ✿ Always remember that friendships are vital parts of who we are. Whatever time we take to invest in them will return a hundred-fold when times are hard.

- ✿ Writing this down tonight has reminded me of the importance of thanking friends and family—even years later for the contributions they make during the tough times in our lives.

- ✿ Stop and ask God to bring someone to mind who has stood by you in the past. Perhaps you can make an effort to let them know how much their kindness has meant to you.

- ✿ When it comes to planning the arrangements for your loved one, don't feel as though you must do what is "expected" in society's eyes. I had a very traditional service because I am very traditional in my likes. You need to do what meets your individual need as a family and what you are comfortable with. However, I would strongly encourage you to plan some time when the people who care about you can come and share that love and concern with you face to face. Even if it is initially hard to face the emotion of seeing people, I believe the end result is very soothing and healing.

NO REGRETS

"I tell you the truth, unless a kernel of wheat falls to the ground and dies, it remains only a single seed. But if it dies, it produces many seeds." (John 12:24, NIV)

The hardest thing to face had finally arrived. I awoke from my restless half-sleep as the sun was coming up. I had barely eaten anything for three days, and yet I found myself so full of tears and sadness that the thought of food didn't even tempt me. When I got up and walked into the kitchen, Gayle's mother tried to persuade me to eat something in her warm, motherly way. I think she would have pretended that the toast was a choo-choo train if she thought it would have made me open my mouth. She was right to say that I needed my strength for the day's events, and truly, I knew that I needed to eat at least a little something to give me some much-needed energy later. I forced down a bite or two—each one sticking in my throat and seeming as if it knew how badly I didn't feel like swallowing it. I remember not wanting to enjoy how food tasted. Have you found that to be true for you? It sounds crazy, but it was almost like if Rick wasn't here to enjoy something good with me, I didn't want to enjoy it either. I bet some of you are nodding your heads again. I felt so many bizarre things like that for quite some time and couldn't help it. None of us can.

After I choked down my breakfast, I went back to Gayle's room and found that it was empty. She was in the bathroom with a friend who was helping her choose what she would wear later that day. Waiting for her to make her decision, I slumped down into a chair and just sat there mentally preparing for my trip back to the funeral home. In some ways I was very anxious to get there and have my time with Rick, and in other ways, I was scared to death. Just then, someone came and told me that they were ready to take us, and so Gayle and I left to take the long ride back downtown.

The first memory I have of stepping back into that room is the overwhelming scent of flowers. The sweet aroma was so concentrated and distinctive that it has left me permanently sensitive to that smell even to this day. I don't think I will ever be able to enjoy carnations ever again. Even the slightest hint of them and suddenly I am back in that room. You, too? I totally understand.

I stood there for a few moments, just looking at all the beautiful arrangements. I was amazed that so many people had sent such beautiful memorials—each one their own gift of love to us. They were truly breathtaking. On some level I was blocking out the fact that Rick's body was in that same room. I was well aware of the casket, but it seemed so impossible, still, that his physical body was just right there if I were to open the lid. Even sitting here typing this out, my hands nearly freeze onto the keyboard as I allow myself to relive that moment in my mind.

The desperation I felt as I came face to face with that flag covered coffin was so consuming. I was completely alone for the very *first* time since the accident had happened and ironically, I was alone with Rick. There was a part of me that came so close to ripping the flag off and opening the casket up...I mean it was all I could do to resist the urge. I had to keep telling myself that I would have been horrified if I did it, but I was horrified anyway. It was torture to know that my eyes had no proof of what I was being told. I struggled with that one issue for a long, long time afterwards. So there I was, spread out over that flag, sobbing and trying to figure out what to do next.

The natural thing was to fall to my knees. Without even realizing it, I sank down onto the floor and simultaneously began conversing with both God and Rick. I would pray a while and then talk a while. I asked God what was happening to me. I told Him I was scared and that I didn't know what to do or where to go or how to act. I began talking to Rick about our life together. I went back and talked about how we met and when we dated. I talked about our wedding and our life together in the military. I told God that I wanted to trust Him through all of this. I laughed at memories we had together with Ben. I cried telling Rick that I didn't know how I'd ever get through Ben's graduation or wedding without him. I asked God to show me where all of this was headed.

    Prayer after prayer, memory after memory, and as this scene unfolded before me I began to see something very clearly. As I brought it into focus its presence nearly took my breath away. In all that time there on my knees what I was doing, in essence, was reliving my whole adult life. It was as authentic a moment as any time in my life—before or since. What I began to see was that although Rick and I certainly didn't *agree* on every single thing, and even though we might have even fussed now and then...the truth was that the story I was reliving there in front of Rick was one that was completely void of any regrets. I didn't find myself sobbing because I had so many things to say I was sorry for, or sobbing because there were things I had never told him, or even sobbing because we had unresolved issues between us. My tears weren't tainted with "what ifs" and "should haves." I realized that if Rick could have sat up and said, "God has given me five more minutes with you." I wouldn't have spent a single one of those minutes fixing something we had neglected to fix before. As I look back, that one realization has brought me more peace and more healing than any other single event during the whole process. Kneeling there, basking in the truth of that moment, I began to pray again. I will never forget that prayer.

Oh God,

I don't even know how to approach You right now. Here I am in the most broken place of my life, and yet I feel You holding me. I feel freedom in knowing that we did all we could to live together for You. Thank You that Rick was that kind of husband and that kind of leader. Thank You that we always took the time to fix it when it was broken and to appreciate it when it wasn't.

I gave Rick's life to You in January, and You knew even then that I would be here on my knees today. I told You then that it would only be by Your grace that I would live through it if You took Rick home early. Well, here I am and I need You to get me through this. I won't make it without You. I choose to give Rick back to You today. I have to because he is Yours and always has been. Thank You for the last eight years of his life and thank You that You knew he needed me for those last eight years, too. It's been a gift to me. Please tell him—and I hope you can hear me, Rick—that the only thing I know to do is to go on being the woman you have always known me to be. I will continue to raise Ben like we have already been doing. I will honor our vows by honoring your memory, and I will try my best to honor you, Rick, and You, God, with the life I live from this point on. So, here he is Lord, take him back and help me to be able to let go.

I love you, Lord Jesus, and I love you, too, Rick.

Amen

I am telling you this with all the sincerity I have inside

me, when I said "Amen" and lifted my head, it was as if I felt the very presence of the Holy Spirit enveloped me. The most liberating, exhilarating breath of air filled my lungs, and I knew that I had been in the very throne room of the Lord. He allowed me the privilege of talking to Rick while praying to Him, and through it I was set free.

Now you may be sitting there crying with me as you realize that you, too, are free from regret. My hopes are that your memories are liberating. If they are, I rejoice with you. However, you may very well be sitting there thinking, "Oh, great. I am *so* happy that you had such a great *freeing* experience. I'm glad you realized that you didn't have any regrets. But, hey, I am *full* of regret. I was left holding a lapful of painful memories, and I really don't care to hear about your wonderful discovery at the foot of Rick's casket. It doesn't help me a bit to know that you found relief while I'm here being eaten up with the pain of all the, 'what ifs' and 'should haves' you mentioned. Thanks a lot, Marlo."

Okay, that is fair, and I told you that we would get to this topic eventually. Well, here it is...we're there.

The truth is that I used to be very torn about sharing this particular part of my experience with others. I felt that the reason I always hesitated was because I knew that many people are often times left with many regrets...and I didn't want to make it worse for them by telling of how wonderful that discovery was for me. I certainly don't want to ever add to anyone's pain.

However, in time, my gradual healing has compelled

me to share it frequently, because it is certainly one of the best life lessons I have ever learned. The lesson is this: we should all purpose to adopt a "no regrets" policy for the remainder of our lives. If you find that you are currently dealing with the Unkind Companion where regret is involved, don't let my words make you feel the worse for it...let them make you feel better.

Always remember that the God we serve is a *forgiving* God and a *restoring* God. You need to realize that when it all comes down to it, it's ultimately a matter of forgiveness. Forgiveness for the one who is gone, forgiveness for yourself, forgiveness between you and God. Let's say that you are carrying around some really valid regrets, and you wish you could tell that certain loved one that you are sorry or that you should have done something differently or that *they* should have done something differently.

My advice to you is this. First, think it through clearly and write it all down. You could even do this in the form of a letter, such as Marilyn Willett Heavilin recommends in her bereavement book, *Roses in December*. Write down every regret that is haunting you and don't stop until you have written *everything* down. Now, read that letter out loud to the person who is gone and don't feel guilty to let all your emotion flow. Don't be soft just because they are dead. I think you should milk every feeling for what it's worth so that when it's put away, it's put away for good. Express whatever it is you want to say to them and then tell them that you forgive them and that you forgive yourself and that you are letting it go.

I would then encourage you earnestly to seek God in prayer, asking Him to restore to you what can only be given back by His grace, and that is *peace*. He absolutely doesn't want you to walk around living on the outside with the gnawing pain of regret killing you on the inside. Let me remind you, though, unless you pray this with your "palms open" it will only come back and bite you at a more opportune time. It is a choice you must make, but I encourage you to make it and be free. I believe with all my heart that grief tied up in regret will never heal. You can't go back and relive the past, but you can make peace with the past, and that's just what God's mercy offers us the ability to do. Accept that gift, and be free.

Once you are liberated from any regret you are carrying, you are then free to live out the rest of your life with a total "no regrets" mentality. I know now through my own experience that I never ever want to take another day for granted. I want the relationships of my inner circle to be lived out in such a way that no untimely death could ever catch me off guard. That kind of living sure takes more effort, but the reward is priceless. Does that mean we will never have problems with others we love? Of course not, because we will always have the flesh to contend with. However, it does mean that we will seek a resolve with those we love as quickly as we can. Even scripture implores us to settle disputes before we go to bed at night. I think this is God's way of saying, "Look, you may not have tomorrow. Take care of this thing tonight, and then you won't have to worry about it any more." It *is* possible to live this way if we are committed to it, and God will help us in our quest. That is the kind of stuff He loves.

— REFLECTIONS —

☙ This issue of regrets is a huge one. It may take you a while to work through it, but the result will be worth all the work. I pray that if you need to let go, you will find the courage to do so. I want you to be free.

☙ Have you found that you have any permanent markers in your life, such as mine with the smell of carnations? How has that affected you? For me, I am very disappointed that I can't enjoy flowers the way I used to. What disappointments do you have?

☙ Is there a loved one that you have unresolved issues with? While you have the chance, make things right with them. We are never promised tomorrow, so take advantage of today.

☙ Notice that I mentioned "palms open" praying again? Remember that I used that term in Chapter Four to express the way I finally approached God with my fear? If we don't come to God with our palms open, we are cheating ourselves of the freedom Christ wants to give us. Be authentic in your prayer life and come to Him with your spiritual hands open wide. He wants to free you.

Were you able to see and touch your loved one after they died? How did that moment make you feel? Comforted? Convinced? Terrified? Frightened? This is something I have struggled with so much. If you were like me, unable to see the body, how has that affected you? Perhaps we have been spared something we don't realize, but I think I will always wish I had been able to touch him one last time.

What a blessed reminder of the truth that we will see our loved ones in Heaven. The next time I see Rick with my eyes, we will both be whole and new. Praise Jesus for this hope! We who are in Christ always have this hope.

CLOSURE

> "The righteous pass away; the godly often die before their time. And no one seems to care or wonder why. No one seems to understand that God is protecting them from the evil to come. For the godly who die will rest in peace." (Isaiah 57:1, NLT)

As we made our way back to the farm to get ready for the service, I rested my head against the car window and watched as the trees streaked by me in a blur. The sky was cloudy and the forecast was calling for scattered storms. I wasn't surprised that it was rainy...I was practically expecting it to be. I felt that maybe God allowed it to be dreary to let me know that He was hurting with us. That may sound silly, but I felt that the weather was His way of letting me know that He knew exactly how I was feeling. He knew that I wasn't up for sunshine.

We arrived back at the farm with only a little while to rest before we had to get dressed to leave. It had not struck me that I hadn't been back in Rick's and my bedroom since the accident happened. I didn't know if I was up for seeing any of his things in our suitcase, but

I longed to feel close to him—mainly because of the horrible time I was having with not being able to see his body. I thought that if I could see something that was his—even if it was just something I had seen him recently wear—that it would make me feel that he was nearby. I knew it would be very emotional, but I decided to do it anyway.

I walked up the stairs and into our room. I quickly discovered that someone had gone through my suitcase and taken all of Rick's things out and put them away. I didn't know whether to feel angry or relieved. I felt like whoever did it knew that at some point I would go up there looking around, and they wanted to prevent me from having to face his stuff being mixed in with mine. I am sure that their intentions were good, but part of me was very disappointed and irritated when his things weren't there. I turned to walk out when suddenly I remembered that Rick had put some things in one of the dressers. I crept over and held my breath as I slid the drawer open and looked inside.

There on the top of the pile was Rick's Bible. My eyes filled with tears as I reached in and took out Rick's most beloved possession. This particular Bible had been a gift from Pop and Gayle when Rick graduated from high school in 1985. He had carried it ever since, and the pages were well worn and full of notes and markings. This Bible was surely one of the most precious and cherished things of Rick's I could have ever come across.

I went directly back down to Gayle's room and shut

the door. As I sat down and opened it, Rick's handwriting reached out and took hold of my spirit. Seeing these personal treasures written by his own hand suddenly filled the room with his presence. How impossible it seemed that the man who had written all those words down was gone for good. I turned to Proverbs 31, where Rick had written in the margins all the qualities he felt that the passage listed for a virtuous wife. At the bottom, he had written in each of the dates that God had confirmed our relationship in his heart. At the very bottom, it said, "3 May, 1988. God has given Marlo to me to be my wife." Tears streamed down my face as I thought about the time I had just spent at the foot of his casket. I spent so much of that time talking to Rick about our relationship, and then I find this precious, romantic reminder of how Rick sought God's will from the very beginning of our life together. It was a painful, yet intimately beautiful gift to give me before the finality of the funeral. This was another tangible reminder that God was, indeed, at work.

 Before we left, we had prayer as a family and asked God to give us strength, and to let the service to be honoring first to Him but also to honor the men that Rick and Pop had been. We also prayed that the Lord would use everything that was said and done to reach those that would be there that didn't know Him as Lord and Savior. We knew that it would be a tremendous opportunity to share His love with all those who came to grieve with us. I knew that Rick would have wanted no less.

Arrival at the church was just as overwhelming as the visitation had been the night before. The outpouring of support was unbelievable, and I only wish they could have all been able to fit into our sanctuary. Many had to go to the overflow facility to watch the service on a screen. I still can't believe how many people came from all over the country to be with us as we said goodbye. My most sincere appreciation is still felt for each family member, serviceman, minister, and friend who helped to make the funeral and burial what it was. I couldn't have done it without each one of you. You know who you are, and I love you.

The funeral, itself, was everything it possibly could have been. There was no word left unsaid, no note left unsung, and no emotion overlooked. God granted us every aspect of the prayer we had offered up before we left the farm. How can I ever adequately express my gratitude for that? I am just thankful that we will have eternity to praise Him! After the healing events of my morning—both the time spent at the funeral home and then my time spent with Rick's Bible—the funeral was very settling for me. I knew that God had already begun the restorative process in my heart, and He confirmed it by the peace in my spirit as the service came to a close and we began our journey back to the farm for the burial. All around us, angels were attending...and it was clear to see the hand of God on the day.

The burial was unlike anything I've ever experienced before or since, in terms of emotion, patriotism, and love. Of course, it was *extremely* difficult to accept the reality that we were getting ready to lay their bodies in the ground, but to be honest, at that particular moment I was as full of pride as I was grief. The overriding energy of the crowd was intensely expectant—an eager anticipation, perhaps, of not knowing what the military involvement would be, but anxious to find out. In our little community, active duty funerals were rare to say the least. The military presence throughout the last few days had been quietly evident. Their "modus operandi" had been very visible but not overpowering. At the burial, however, all that changed.

Both Daddy and the military liaisons worked tirelessly to pull it all together in just three days, and what they ultimately were able to do was incredible. All of their faithful dedication resulted in a tribute more perfect than anything I could have planned had I been given three months to prepare—much less three days. All of the characteristics unique to the tradition are breathtaking, but when the airmen from Rick's former C-130 squadron from Pope AFB made the unprecedented request to do a missing man formation over the farm...well, it just sent the moment right over the top. As they roared overhead, the ground shook with fierce vibrations of intimate brotherhood. It took tremendous will to stare into that missing man configuration, knowing just whose airplane was represented by the eerie void. However, painful as it was to watch, I couldn't take my eyes off of it. I fixed my gaze on the horizon and watched until the fractured pattern was reduced to nothing more than thin air. It was a gift beyond compare.

As difficult as that was to take in, I think that the *most* difficult part for me, personally, was at the end when I was presented with the folded flag and those famous military words, "Mrs. Peddycord, on behalf of a grateful nation, we salute you." It was then that the bugler began his rendition of *Taps*. The notes cut me like a knife, and I looked up into the face of the young man who was handing me the flag. He had one single tear rolling down his cheek, and when I saw that, I fell apart. How profound that image was, and still is, in my mind.

I stood to my feet and approached the casket for one last goodbye. Once more, I lay over on it and kissed it, whispering, "I love you, Rick, and I'll always miss you." Benjamin followed close beside me, his little hand clasped tight around mine, and we took the first steps of the rest of our lives, together. As we emerged from the tent and stepped out into the open, for just a brief second or two, the clouds parted and the sun shined down on us bright and warm. I remember lifting my head and feeling the glow on my face; its brilliance giving me just the energy I needed to face the receiving line once again. I was later to learn that those brief seconds of sunshine were an answered prayer for Mama. I'll tell you about it some other time because it is a great story. You'll love it.

I have spent much time since trying to figure out how it was we were given such a grand farewell at the farm that day when so much should have prevented it working out. The *only* explanation I have ever been able to come up with is that God simply chose to honor Rick's life because Rick chose to honor God.

This may seem an odd place to draw this first book to a close, but I think not. We have just spent some very valuable time walking through the first and most gripping moments of the grieving process together. For each one of us, these first few days are so amazingly surreal, just getting through the funeral is an amazing accomplishment. If you have made it this far then you are still hanging in there, and that is something of which you should be very proud. Some people *don't* make it this far...so if you have, you should not underestimate what a powerful achievement it is. You may be far from where you want to be, and hopefully, far from where you will be, but thank God you're here!

As we begin to bring this all full-circle, I want to go ahead and lay the groundwork for the time we'll spend together in the future. I want to give you some things to think about until we come back to look closely at what happens when the adrenaline starts to wear off. What happens when the casseroles quit showing up at the door and the mailbox gathers cobwebs? Until that time, I want you to think about where *this* story leaves us. Remember all the times in this book that I've made reference to the Unkind Companion? If you will recall, that is the title I gave you at the beginning of this book for the term *loss*. I named it the Unkind Companion because when it invades your world, it is as if it's a living entity. It imposes itself upon you and suddenly you are forced to make room for it, and not only that, but it takes over every part of your life for an indefinite amount of time. I believe that the effect it has on you will lead you one of two ways.

The first possibility is that you will go through the shock of the experience and make it through the best way you know how. In the days, weeks, and months that follow, you'll discover that your healing isn't going very well. The pain isn't subsiding at all, and your thoughts begin to turn angry and hard. You may find that you begin to blame God, or yourself, for what has happened. You just want to blame someone. You stop talking about your loss, and you push others away. You refuse to move forward with your life and become irritated at anyone or anything that would encourage you to do otherwise. It won't be long before your life doesn't seem to count for much, and you begin to view the whole world with cynicism and doubt. This, dear friends, is exactly the effect Satan wants the Unkind Companion to have on you. If he can convince you that what you've been through is too much to overcome, then he will start trying to convince you that you don't want to live either. If he accomplishes that, then he has won.

The alternative to that is what I hope for you and infinitely more, what God hopes for you. When the Unkind Companion comes calling, you find that you are helpless to prevent it. Like in scenario number one, you make it through the shock of the experience the best way you know how. It is there, however, that the similarity ends. In the days, weeks, and months that follow, you will discover that you are hurting beyond belief, but your heart cries out to God for comfort. You turn to Him for your strength, and you realize that some days you can only handle five minutes at the time, but by His grace, you handle it. You purpose your heart to move forward in life, knowing that it is okay to ask God why, but keeping a soft heart in His presence as He answers you. You choose to keep on living in order to honor God, but also to honor the memory of the one you loved. You realize that they would want you to move on with your living. You believe that moving on doesn't mean you are forgetting your loved one, and so you step out into the freedom that realization brings with your hand wrapped tightly around the Father's. You learn, through much hard work and suffering that you can ultimately make peace with this Unkind Companion that has set up residence in your life. It will never go away, but you *can* learn to live together within the same heart.

It is at this point that your loss can become something usable. Instead of the empty dregs of bitterness that Satan will offer you, you can choose to walk in the freedom of Christ with your loss transformed into an effective experience. A few years ago, I read a quote by a man named Dan Allender. It touched me in such a profound way, and I think it states so well what I am trying to say to you. It said:

Allow the pain of the past and the travail of the change process to create fresh new life in you and to serve as a bridge over which another victim my cross from death to life.

I would like to go back and share with you something Daddy said to me immediately following the funeral. His words were centered on this idea of the "fresh new life" to which I believe Dan Allender was speaking. We were sitting in the limousine outside the church. Daddy turned to face me and he said,

"Marlo, I want to tell you something. Over the last few days I have been doing all the busy work. I've wanted to help get everything settled for you as quickly as I could, but in doing that, I haven't had much time to sit and talk with you. Looking at you, I keep thinking of what happens when you chop down a tree. You see, chopping down a dead tree and chopping down a live tree are two *totally* different things. Initially, they both look the same. All you can see sticking up out of the ground is a lifeless stump. You assume that it's all over. For the dead tree, it is. But, for the live tree, it's only temporary. If the roots of the live tree aren't damaged when the cut is made, then when enough time has passed, little green shoots will start springing up all over the place. Before you know it, it looks like a bush is growing right up out of the top of the stump. It just goes to show that you can't judge what is coming by what you see. I know that for you, you feel like you have been truncated. You feel like this accident has come along and cut you off at your base. In a way, you feel dead, yourself. However, I believe that your roots have not been damaged and when enough time has passed, God is going to let new life come out of where you have been cut. You have to hold onto that and believe it. Your life is not over because your *roots* are *alive*."

―――

It is *my* prayer that in time, you will have new life springing from where *you* have been truncated. Don't be rushed, for it *will* take time to reach this end. There are no short cuts to healing. I would suggest using this dormant time to tend to your roots and to wait for God's divine leading as you move ahead. Don't let your loved one's passing be for nothing. Ask God to use *you* to make their life count for something, and then watch in amazement as He brings it to pass.

If our roots are grounded by the streams of Living Water, we will emerge from these dark days full of new life—well-equipped to offer the next victim of loss the encouragement of our own personal experience. By it, may they find the bridge *they* have been searching for to begin that difficult crossing-over for themselves. I want to leave you with this challenge: Always remember...if you will trust God today, He can take your yesterday and bless someone else's tomorrow. In that, there is everlasting hope and victory for us all!

May you be blessed as you step out to begin your own personal journey.

The End

No...

THE BEGINNING, AGAIN